God Speaks to Me, Too

A Spiritual Memoir

Patrick J. Delohery

For Adam

July 15, 1991 – February 18, 2018

"Of course, it was Adam."

Prologue

There is a particular loneliness that belongs exclusively to people who have heard God speak.

Not the loneliness of isolation — you may be surrounded by family, by friends, by a congregation of people who love you and mean you well. The loneliness I am describing is more precise than that. It is the loneliness of having experienced something so real, so specific, so unmistakably present that you know it happened — and then discovering, over the course of your life, that most of the frameworks available to you for understanding what happened were built by people who either never had the experience themselves, or who had it and were afraid to say so plainly.

I am not afraid to say so plainly. God has spoken to me. Jesus has spoken to me. The Holy Spirit has moved through me in ways I can describe but never fully convey. An Archangel has stood beside me — at least twice, separated by more than forty years.

I am sixty-eight years old. I have been an electrical engineer for over thirty-five years. The first microchip I designed now runs in more than five million deployed systems, still at the original and only revision. I have been named inventor on multiple U.S. and foreign patents. I have spent my professional life in the world of measurable signal, verifiable data, and reproducible results. I do not say these things to impress you. I say them because you deserve to know who is talking to you, and what kind of mind is making these claims.

The title of this book is not a metaphor. It is not an invitation to pretend, or to project, or to interpret natural events as divine ones. It is a statement of fact, and it is addressed directly to you — because I believe, with everything in me, that God speaks to you, too. Perhaps you already know it. Perhaps you have felt it and had no language for it or have been made to feel foolish for believing it. Perhaps you are sitting with a grief so large right now that the question of whether God exists has become brutally personal. Wherever you are, that is exactly where this book is meant to find you.

This is a spiritual memoir. It is the record of a life spent in a deeply personal relationship with God — a relationship that began when I was ten years old, watching my brother attempt to murder my other brother with a shotgun I brought to their fistfight. A relationship that deepened in the dark, under a moonless Colorado sky when I was seventeen, in a circle of Gamble Oak, pouring everything in my mind onto the pages of a spiral notebook until my thoughts ran out, and God spoke into the silence. A relationship that was tested to its foundation by my own failure, withdrawn with surgical precision, and then restored — on the exact anniversary of my transgression — through a message delivered by an Archangel.

I am not writing a theology. I am not proposing a new religion, starting a movement, or asking you to agree with every conclusion I have reached. Some of what I say about institutional Christianity, about the history of the Bible, about original sin and the nature of God, will trouble some readers. I understand that. I am not writing to trouble you. I am writing to tell you the truth as I have lived it — because the truth as I have lived it is that God is far larger, far more personal, and far more directly accessible than most of the institutions built in His name have been willing to tell you.

God does not live inside a denomination. He does not require a hierarchy to reach you. He does not deal in the currency of fear and eternal damnation with the children He created in His own image and likeness. He deals in love — specific, present, occasionally astonishing, always faithful love — and He speaks in whatever language will reach you. He spoke to a seventeen-year-old in the language of the cosmos, pointing at the Milky Way and saying simply, "There ya go, lad." He spoke to me in a chapel in Colorado Springs in the voice of an old friend who was glad to see me. He spoke to me in the silence after the worst loss of my life, when He reminded me of a promise I had made and a caveat I had attached to it and showed me that what I said I could not survive was precisely what I was surviving.

Two words define the operating system of man's relationship with God. Personal accountability. I arrived at those two words at the age of twelve, through a comparative religious studies curriculum I designed myself — a curriculum that examined most major non-satanic religions on earth and asked a single organizing question: what do they all agree on? They agreed on two things: That there is a God, or some creative force greater than man. And every person is personally accountable, to God, for their actions and inactions in this life. Hindus and Buddhists call it karma. Jews say you reap what you sow. Christians say cast your bread on the water, and it will surely return to you. Two words. The entire framework. Elegant and manageable and just.

I have lived those two words in ways I could not have imagined at twelve. I have been held accountable with a precision that still takes my breath away. I have also been forgiven with a mercy so specific, so perfectly timed, that it could only have come from the God who was counting the years from the first moment of my failure.

That is what this book is about. It is about the night of July 26, 1974, and what happened to a seventeen-year-old boy in the dark. It is about an Archangel at sunrise and a conversation with Jesus in a pew in a Catholic chapel. It is about my son Adam, who left this world at twenty-six, and the words I said when I heard the news — words I did not understand at the time but understood completely five years later. It is about the architecture of a life in God's company — which is not always a comfortable life, or a perfect one, but is a life in which you are never, in any ultimate sense, alone.

If you are someone who has walked away from organized religion but has not walked away from God — this is for you.

If you are someone who has had experiences, you cannot explain and cannot forget — this is for you.

If you are sitting in grief right now, wondering where God is — this is especially for you.

He is closer than you think. He has always been closer than you think.

God speaks to me. He speaks to you, too. I am certain of it.

Chapter 1

Divine Intervention

I was ten years old, when God made his divine love and Grace known to me.

One afternoon, I came home from school to find my oldest brother sitting on my other brother's chest, pinning his shoulders to the floor with his knees, and beating him with a relentless, methodical ferocity that I hadn't ever seen from him before. Jim was fifteen — tall, strong, and genuinely enraged. Tom had just turned thirteen, was four-foot-eleven, and — to be charitable — rotund. Apparently, something Tom said about Jim's girlfriend had lit the fuse that escalated into the mayhem I suddenly found myself in the middle of.

Growing up in Denver in the 1960s, my brothers and I hunted and fished the Colorado Rockies from the time we could carry a rifle. We had grown up around firearms. Each of us had our own guns in the basement of our house on South Xavier Street, and we knew how to handle them. Not knowing what else to do in that moment, that is where I went — downstairs, straight to Tom's 16-gauge, single-shot shotgun.

Unsure of my ability to bluff my oldest brother out of his rage with an empty shotgun, I put a shell in the chamber, closed the breech and returned to the room where they were fighting. I put the barrel of the gun behind Jim's left ear, pulled back the hammer and, in the most serious voice I could manufacture, said: "Get off him or I'll blow your head off!" Jim stopped immediately. He raised both hands, stood slowly, and backed away from Tom, keeping his eyes on me the entire time.

"Are we good?" Jim asked, hoping for confirmation that he had fully complied with my demand.

"Yeah," I said. "We're good," and we were, for three or four seconds.

Then Tom came off the floor.

He grabbed the shotgun out of my hands, shoved me aside, put the barrel point-blank in Jim's now horrified face...and pulled the trigger.

What happened in the three or four seconds between the time Tom jumped to his feet, leveled that shotgun at our older brother, and pulled the trigger is something I have thought about more times than I can count across the fifty-eight years since.

Time did not merely slow down. It expanded — the way it does when traumatic events occur and everything that matters is suddenly, completely on the line. Three or four seconds stretched into what seemed like minutes. The room went still in a way that had nothing to do with quiet. I was being held, in a kind of suspended animation — motionless, aware with an extraordinary, almost preternatural clarity, watching what was unfolding before me from what felt like a great, calm height.

And in those expanded seconds, before the trigger was ever pulled, a realization arrived with a certainty that simply could not be denied - a miracle was occurring. Not had occurred. Was occurring — in real time - as the Holy Spirit held me, I watched God demonstrate His profound love for my brothers and me - and we all had just experienced His divine Grace.

The miracle I was experiencing actually began some 15 to 20 seconds earlier, before I re-entered the room where Tom was being pummeled. As I was running back up the stairs, with the loaded shotgun in hand, I was stopped. Not by hesitation, not by second thoughts — physically stopped, mid-step, in a way that had absolutely no natural explanation. For perhaps five seconds I stood there, held by a force that was not my own, in a stillness that did not belong to me. And in that stillness, a command arrived — not a suggestion, not a prompting, not a whisper, but an absolute and non-negotiable demand, carrying the full authority of something infinitely larger than a ten-year-old boy on a staircase in Denver:

"Remove the shell before you go back into that room." I followed the command, ejected the shell, put it in my pocket, closed the breech then hurried back up the stairs.

Now, standing very still in the middle of that room, in the aftermath of all that had just happened, one thing ran through my mind with quiet, overwhelming force:

"Mom! You're right! There IS a God, and He just saved Jim's life!"

My saintly mother, Dorothy Delohery, had been telling her 6 children there was a God for as long as any of us could remember — in the Irish-Catholic way, which involves equal parts prayer, pragmatism, and the unspoken assumption that God is simply part of the household, present and paying attention, whether acknowledged or not. She had been right all along. Now, for me, there was simply no question about it. There never would be again.

Here is what that afternoon settled, and what it did not.

It settled that God was real. That the Holy Spirit was real — real in the specific, physical sense of having will and presence and the authority to stop a boy on a flight of stairs with a direct and non-negotiable command. The faith I had been raised in was pointing at something true.

What it did not settle was whether everything else that faith claimed was equally true. The doctrine. The institutional claims. The hierarchy. The God who had stopped me on those stairs required no priest, no sacrament, no ecclesiastical apparatus of any kind. He simply arrived and acted — with the directness of a parent pulling a child back from the edge of a road, at the moment it mattered most.

That was not the God of the catechism class. The God in catechism was administered, dispensed through proper channels, available by appointment. The God on those stairs was immediate. He did not wait for the appropriate process. He showed up, uninvited by any institution, on a staircase in southwest Denver, and He stopped a ten-year-old boy from carrying a loaded shotgun into a room where it would have dramatically, and tragically, changed everything that came after.

And so it was, at ten years old, the most important question of my life had just presented itself — not what I had been taught, but what was actually true. I began searching for that answer later that afternoon. What I found is the subject of a later chapter.

But it started there, on those stairs, in a room where my brother had just survived what should have been his last moment on earth — because something, or someone, stopped me and demanded I remove that shell before I walked back into that room.

Fifty-eight years later, the gratitude for that demand, and my compliance with it, has never diminished. Not for a second.

Tom went on to earn a master's degree in Cellular and Molecular Radiation Biology from Colorado State University. He spent more than thirty-five years at the cutting edge of cancer research at Memorial Sloan-Kettering Cancer Center and other world-class research institutions in and around New York City. He devoted his professional life to the fight against one of the cruelest diseases in the human catalogue. He may well have saved many lives.

Jim lives with his wife in the foothills of Mount Evans in Colorado, at about 9,000 feet elevation. Retired now. If he's not out hunting or fishing, or wrenching on his 66' Camaro, he's most likely with his grandkids.

My brothers and I came within an empty chamber of losing everything. All three of us got to live our lives fully. I thank God for that every day, and I thank Him for the command on those stairs — the five seconds that changed everything that came after.

Chapter 2

The Quest

Two years after those stairs, I was twelve years old and in seventh grade at Kunsmiller Junior High School in southwest Denver. The questions that afternoon had planted in me had been growing the entire time, quietly and insistently, the way questions do when they matter enough. I had finally reached the point where something systematic had to be done about it.

What I knew for certain: God was real. The Holy Spirit was real — real in the immediate, physical sense of having will and presence and the authority to stop a boy on a staircase with a non-negotiable command. That was established beyond any possibility of revision. What was not established was what it meant in the context of everything else I had been taught. Was the

God on those stairs the God of the Roman Catholic Church specifically? Of Christianity broadly? Or was He something larger, older, and far less denominational than any institution ever built in His name?

To find out, I designed a curriculum.

A Comparative Religious Studies course — structured to examine the world's major non-satanic religions in turn: their histories, their founding narratives, their core beliefs, their understanding of God and of man's relationship to God. The course was built around one specific organizing question: was there a common thread running through all of them? The reasoning behind the question was simple. If God was real and present in human experience across all of history and all cultures, then some trace of that reality should be detectable in every sincere human attempt to describe and relate to Him, regardless of what name that attempt operated under, regardless of what century or continent produced it.

I took the curriculum to my 7th grade Social Studies teacher, Lee Regan. He listened carefully, told me that a public school could not formally offer a religious studies course, but said he believed he could find a way to make it work. He presented it to the appropriate school officials as an after-hours elective for extra credit, and it was approved. Seventh and eighth grade students were invited to enroll. Twelve to fifteen of them did.

Lee Regan deserves more than a passing mention here. He was a Social Studies teacher at Kunsmiller; a public junior high school in southwest Denver. He could have done any number of things with a twelve-year-old who showed up with a ten-week comparative religious studies course he'd designed himself. He could have redirected me, gently or otherwise. He could have sent me to the guidance counselor. Instead, he looked at what was genuinely being attempted and found a way to help it happen. That is a teacher doing his job at the highest level, and I have been grateful for that for more than fifty years.

The ten week course covered Hinduism, Buddhism, Judaism, Christianity, and several other traditions. Each was examined on its own terms — not as a curiosity or a competitor to the faith I had been raised in, but as a serious and sincere human effort to understand the nature of God and the nature of the relationship between God and man. What each tradition said about creation. What each said about the soul. What each said about the obligations of a human life. What each said about what happens when that life ends.

At the end of the ten weeks, one question was put to the students: what, if anything, is the common thread — or threads — that run through the world's major non-satanic religions?

Every student in the class answered in essentially the same way.

First: there is a God, or some creative force greater than man. Second: every person is personally accountable to God for their actions and inactions in this life.

That is it. Two words. The entire shared foundation of every major faith tradition on earth, distilled by a room full of seventh and eighth graders in southwest Denver. Different traditions express it differently — the Hindus and Buddhists speak of karma, the perfect and impersonal accounting of cause and effect that follows every human action through every lifetime. The Jews say you reap what you sow. The Christians say cast your bread on the water, and it will surely return to you. The language varies enormously. The underlying claim is identical. There is a God. And every one of us is personally accountable to Him for how we live.

Two words. Personal accountability. The entire operating system of man's relationship with God, in two words. No elaborate doctrine required. No institutional hierarchy necessary. No threat of eternal damnation for those born in the wrong place or the wrong century. A basic rule and a basic expectation, extended to all of God's children everywhere, in every time and place they have ever lived. Simple. Elegant. And once you see it, impossible to unsee.

What God taught me at twelve — not through a priest, not through catechism, but through careful study and a room full of curious students following a question honestly to its conclusion — was something that no religious institution had been eager to say aloud: there is no "True Religion." There cannot be. God and the Holy Trinity exist completely outside the manmade concept of religion. They precede it, transcend it, and are in no way contained or defined by it. Religion is what human beings construct to organize their experience of something they can feel but never fully capture, something that is always larger than the vessel built to hold it. At its best, it provides community, moral structure, and historical memory. At its worst, it positions itself as the required gateway between you and the God who was already reaching for you before the first institution was ever built.

God does not live in a denomination. He was here before all of them. He will be here long after every one of them has changed beyond recognition or passed from the earth entirely.

I was twelve years old when that understanding arrived. I have never had reason to revise it in the fifty-six years since.

A word about institutional Christianity specifically, because some of what follows in this book will challenge some readers, and I want the context established clearly before going further.

Christianity and the Christian ethic are held here in deep reverence. The foundational moral framework of Western Civilization, and America itself, is established in, and by, the Christian ethic. My parents' Catholic faith was one of the great stabilizing influences of my childhood. My mother's faith was real, it was lived, and it produced a woman of extraordinary character. I would not trade any of it.

What I reject, precisely and specifically, are particular institutional doctrines that do not survive basic logical scrutiny and are, in several important cases, historically manufactured. That is not opposition to faith. It is the application of intellectual honesty to questions that deserve it. God gave me a mind. In my experience, He has always been pleased when I use it.

No Protestant church would exist today without the Roman Catholic Church. Not one. The Church alone held all the source documents — the works and writings of all the disciples, including Mary Magdalene, Thomas, Judas, and others — through three hundred years of Christian persecution before the Nicene Council was convened. Every Protestant denomination that has ever existed, or ever will, built its theology on documents translated, curated, and canonized by that Council. This is documented history. It is almost never acknowledged in Protestant discourse, and that silence is not accidental.

The Nicene Council was convened, managed, and overseen by the Roman Emperor Constantine in approximately 325 AD. This is the same man who executed his oldest son, Crispus, on suspicion of having an affair with his stepmother, then executed his second wife Fausta, who had brought the accusation. This is the man under whose editorial authority the foundational document of modern Christianity was assembled, curated, and published. Not a controversial claim. A documented historical fact. Anyone reading the Bible without that knowledge is reading without essential context.

The translation process introduced layers of human interpretation that cannot be set aside. The source texts were in Hebrew, Latin, and Aramaic. The first New Testament was assembled in Greek. When translators encountered words in the source languages with no direct Greek equivalent — and there were many, particularly in the Aramaic texts recording what Jesus actually said — members of the Council made choices. Human choices, shaped by theological commitment, political pressure, and the particular biases of men living in the fourth century, always in service of the canonical narrative being shaped under Constantine's direction.

Jesus spoke in Aramaic — a language of parables and layered meaning in which the literal surface of a statement is always pointing at something deeper - never intending to have but one interpretation. When Jesus said, "no one comes to the Father except through me," institutional Christianity interprets that as an exclusive legal claim. To paraphrase, conscious belief in Jesus as the Son of God is the only path to salvation, and every human being outside that specific confession is condemned to eternal damnation.

Consider carefully what that interpretation actually requires. It condemns every person who lived before Jesus was born. It condemns every person in the vast portions of the world that Christianity never reached in any meaningful way. It condemns every sincere, God-fearing human being across all of human history who honored God under a different name but who lived in personal accountability — the universal principle that every major faith tradition independently recognizes. The God of unconditional love, the God I have spoken with personally, did not design a system that condemns billions of His children for the crime of being born in the wrong time or the wrong place. Taken as the Aramaic parable it was always intended to be, "through me" means through the light, the love, the divine nature that Jesus embodied — and that exists as a living possibility within every human soul. That reading makes it the most inclusive statement in the New Testament. The literal reading makes it the most exclusive. Fifty-eight years of a direct, personal relationship with the God that statement is describing, informs me of which one I believe is true.

And then there is original sin.

The doctrine of original sin holds that all of humanity is permanently tainted by the choices of Adam and Eve in the Garden of Eden, and that this inherited guilt requires the redemptive sacrifice of Christ to address. Without original sin, the institution's primary mechanism of control — the claim that Jesus' sacrifice was necessary to redeem the accumulated debt of all humanity — becomes very difficult to justify. Which is precisely why the institution needs it, and why it has defended it so vigorously for so long.

But consider what the doctrine is actually claiming: that a son should be held permanently accountable for the choices of a father he never met, for a transgression that occurred before he existed, in which he had no voice and no part. That a child enters the world already carrying a debt she had no hand in incurring and cannot undo. In any other context — in any system of law in any civilized nation on earth — this would be recognized instantly as obviously and indefensibly unjust. God is the author of justice. He is the source and definition of what is fair and right. The suggestion that God would construct a system He Himself would recognize as unjust is not a difficult theological problem. It is an incoherent one.

Babies and very young children have always responded to me with a particular warmth and calm recognition — looking at me the way you look at an old, familiar friend. I have observed this countless times across a lifetime. Babies arrive from God. They are with Him before they are born. They carry His light into the world, as yet undimmed by everything the world will later work to diminish. They do not arrive full of sin. They arrive full of God. Original sin is the institutional mechanism that inverts that truth, manufacturing a debt that only the institution can then address. You do not need to be "born again". God does not need a do-over. You were born precisely when and as God intended for you to be born. He is God. He doesn't make mistakes.

None of this makes me anti-Christian or anti-religion. These are the conclusions of a man who has lived in direct, personal, and ongoing relationship with God for fifty-eight years, and who holds himself to the same standard of intellectual honesty he applied to everything else across a long engineering career. I offer them not as doctrine but as testimony. You are free to reach your own conclusions. God gave you a mind, too.

Chapter 3

Growing Up in America

To understand the night of July 26, 1974, and why it meant what it meant to me, you need to understand the world that produced it.

I was born on June 9th, 1957 — the ninth day of the sixth month, the third son of my father. The significance of those numbers would take decades to reveal itself. The youngest of six children, I grew up in southwest Denver in a household where the news was always on, both parents had strong opinions, and those opinions collided at the dinner table with the kind of conviction that only an Irish-Catholic family can sustain indefinitely without anyone actually changing their mind. My father was a Republican. My mother was a Democrat. Both were devoted Catholics. Both were news junkies. The table was never quiet.

My father, Martin J. Delohery, was 100 percent Irish and first-generation American. His parents had emigrated from Ireland around 1917 and settled in Chicago, bringing with them the particular combination of stubbornness, humor, deep faith, and absolute refusal to be pushed around that seems to be standard equipment for people from that island. He was a businessman and an entrepreneur who managed an FW Woolworth store with the kind of dignity and genuine community investment that made it more than a retail operation. He knew his customers. He knew their families. He cared about both. He was active in the Republican Party, deeply proud of his Irish heritage, and a man whose word, once given, was the most reliable thing in any room he occupied. I have never known a more principled man. He was my first and most enduring model of what integrity looks like in practice, and I have spent my adult life in sincere — not always successful — pursuit of that standard.

My mother was half Irish, half Austrian, and entirely Catholic — in the way that only a woman can be all of those things simultaneously, which is to say with great warmth, considerable authority, and an absolute certainty about the things that mattered most. She was the spiritual center of the household in the way that mothers often are, whether anyone acknowledges it or not. Both families had been Catholic for hundreds of years. Their faith was not just a Sunday obligation in our house. It was the foundation around which everything else was organized - the first language of comfort and accountability alike.

As alluded to earlier, both of my parents were news junkies. The television or radio was always on, always tuned to what was happening. The consequence was that I absorbed the events of the 1960s and early 1970s not as historical facts to be studied later, but as present reality — experienced in real time, around a dinner table, by people who were genuinely paying attention and genuinely moved by what they were watching. I did not learn about those years in a classroom. I lived them, in a living room on South Xavier Street, through the voices of Walter Cronkite and Huntley-Brinkley and the glow of our black-and-white Zenith television.

The world, in those years, was doing its level best to come apart.

I was six years old when a nun at St. Mary's Catholic Elementary School in Wichita, Kansas — where my father was managing a Woolworth store at the time — sent us home early one Friday afternoon in November of 1963. Sister Mary George told our class, with a composure that I still remember, that President Kennedy had been shot in Dallas, and that we should go home to be with our families.

I went home to find both of my parents sobbing in front of the television.

My father was not a man who cried. He was Irish to his bones — tough in the specific way that people are tough when they come from a people who have survived famine and brutal occupation, for centuries, and who intend to survive whatever comes next. I had never seen him cry. That afternoon, he was weeping. My mother was weeping. The television was on, and no one was speaking. The whole room felt wrong in a way I had no words for.

President Kennedy was, for our family, one of our own. The first Irish-Catholic President of the United States. A genuine hero of World War II — the man who saved his crew after PT-109 was rammed and sunk in the Pacific by a Japanese destroyer, who swam through miles an open ocean with an injured man in tow, who had shown that an Irish-Catholic boy from Boston could sit in the highest office in the land and conduct himself with intelligence, grace, and genuine dignity. For an Irish-Catholic family in 1963, the loss of John Fitzgerald Kennedy was not a political event. It was like experiencing a death in the family - a story, and a legacy, left unfulfilled.

It was the first and last time I ever saw my father cry.

As it turned out, JFK was only the first of a series of political assassinations. Malcolm X was assassinated in February of 1965. Martin Luther King was shot on the balcony of the Lorraine Motel in Memphis in April of 1968. Bobby Kennedy — Jack's younger brother, who had just won the California Democratic primary and was on his way to what many believed was an inevitable presidency — was shot in the kitchen of the Ambassador Hotel in Los Angeles just two months after King. Four political assassinations in five years. Four men who had, in their different ways, represented something people believed in. A country that could land men on the moon apparently could not protect the people standing at its podiums.

Vietnam ground on with no end in sight, consuming the older brothers of boys and girls I knew and delivering body counts to American living rooms with the regularity of a weather report. The numbers climbed. The justifications grew thinner. The photographs grew harder to look at. In May of 1970, National Guardsmen shot and killed four students at Kent State University in Ohio who were protesting the bombing of Cambodia. Four students. On an American college campus. Shot by American soldiers in American uniforms. The country argued about whether the students deserved it.

The riots in Watts. The burning of American cities in the summer of 1967. The Democratic National Convention in Chicago in 1968 — the police and the protesters and the whole catastrophe broadcast live, the world watching. The Chicago 7 trial that followed. Night after night, year after year, all of it came into the living room.

I was five years old when I sat beside my mother and watched Bull Connor turn fire hoses and attack dogs on little children in Birmingham, Alabama simply for the color of their skin. Too young to understand the full politics. Not too young to be physically sickened by it. Those images — the firehoses, the dogs, the children being blown down the street like tumbleweeds with water pressure so strong it could tear the bark off trees — have never left me. They were my first understanding that the world contained a category of evil that wore the uniform of authority and called itself justice, and that this category was not a relic of some other time. It was present. It was now. It was happening on American streets, in front of American cameras, in the American South that was not that far from Wichita, Kansas - where I lived at the time.

That was the world pressing in from all sides on a seventeen-year-old boy on a Colorado hillside on the night of July 26, 1974. The backdrop against which every question about the future had to be honestly answered. Not as abstraction — as lived experience. I had grown up watching the world crack and been formed by it, in ways I was only beginning to understand that summer.

Chapter 4

The Night Everything Changed

Seven years after those stairs, the summer of 1974 — and a completely different kind of crisis.

July 25th started at Mile High Stadium in Denver, at the Crosby, Stills, Nash, and Young reunion tour concert. Tens of thousands of people, extraordinary music, the kind of warm Colorado summer event that makes you feel like anything is possible. It should have been one of the great days of that summer - but my heart was heavy. It had been for weeks.

There was a girl. Her name in not important - but the impact she ultimately had no my life cannot be overstated. She was beautiful and kind, and I was completely in love with her in the way that only a seventeen-year-old boy can be in love — fully, without reservation, without the protective layers that experience eventually builds. A few weeks earlier she had broken up with me and gone back to her previous boyfriend, a methamphetamine addict who had, deliberately by my reckoning, drawn her into the same addiction he suffered from and gotten her pregnant. The following day, she was to marry him.

Being the youngest of six — three older sisters, two older brothers — I had been thoroughly counseled by my mother and sisters on how a young man ought to treat a girl he cared about: keep your hands to yourself, honor her, demonstrate through restraint that she matters to you as a person. So deeply in love with this girl, I had listened faithfully. I never even kissed her during the short time we were together. Unfortunately, she broke up with me partly for that reason — she needed warmth and affection that my sincere compliance with my family's guidance had withheld. My restraint cost me the relationship. She went back to a man who offered something very different, and the trajectory of her life after that choice was not what it should have been. There was nothing I could have done to change it. But understanding that and making peace with it are two different things, and on the night of July 25th, I had not yet made peace.

My dear mother picked me up after the concert from a friend's house. We arrived home around 1:30 in the morning of July 26th. I said goodnight to her, grabbed a spiral notebook and a pen, and went back outside. My three-legged German Shepherd, Zeus, came with me.

Out on the property, there was a spot I went when I needed to think and pray alone — an open area, completely encircled by Gamble Oak, far enough from the lights of Denver and Castle Rock that the sky looked the way it was always meant to look. It was a beautiful, moonless morning. I settled in and looked up, and there was the Milky Way running directly overhead, north to south, edge to edge across the entire sky. A river of light, impossibly vivid, the kind of sky that makes you feel both very small and very held at the same time.

I tried to begin sorting through everything pressing down on me and immediately encountered a problem: there were too many thoughts competing at the same moment to make sense of any single one. Every time my mind reached for the girl, it got

Vietnam. Every time it reached for the future, it collided with the present. Every time it tried to find God in the middle of all of it, everything arrived at once and nothing resolved.

So I made a decision. Every single thought crossing my mind was going down on paper — legible or not, organized or not, one thought written directly over the last — until the notebook held everything and my mind held nothing. Writing in the dark, on uneven ground, neatly was not possible. Writing happened anyway. Thought over thought over thought, whatever came, without editing or ordering, just emptying — until the noise began, gradually, to still.

The act of emptying everything onto paper created the clarity needed to actually address what mattered most. The mind, once drained of accumulated, unprocessed noise, could finally focus on a single thing at a time.

First, I focused on the girl and my broken heart. Her beautiful face, her laughter, her marriage later that morning to a man who was not worthy of her - her unborn daughter. I sat with it honestly, made peace with what could not be changed, and resolved to support her no matter what followed. I resolved to pray for her and her daughter, to never stop loving her, and I kept that resolution — through all the years that followed — in the quiet way that kept promises operate, without announcement.

With that settled, thoughts turned to the future. To the world I had grown up in. The assassinations. Vietnam. Kent State. The first and last time I had ever seen my father cry. All of it was present with me in that circle of Gamble Oak, under that sky, at two in the morning — the full weight of the era I had come of age in, the backdrop against which the question of what my own life was going to be - had to be answered.

And then, thinking about a family someday — about children, about the kind of father I wanted to be and the kind of human beings I wanted to raise — something crystallized. The world desperately needed more good people. If God were to grant me children, I would do everything in my power to raise the best human beings I possibly could. That was the commitment.

So I made a promise to God. Said directly, the way you make a commitment to someone you trust completely: if You grant me children, dear God, I will do everything in my power to raise them well. God-centered. With a foundation the world cannot take away from them.

Then I added a caveat.

Said it honestly, from the deepest place I understood about myself at seventeen: God, please never take any of my children from me, because I don't think I could ever deal with losing a child.

I believed that completely. Sitting there under those stars with Zeus beside me and the notebook on my lap, I believed it with everything I had. I told God the one thing I could not survive.

He heard it. He noted it. The full weight of those words would not become clear to me for more than forty years.

Right after making that promise, a very practical realization followed — because that is how my mind has always worked. Providing for the family I had just asked God for was going to require a well-paying career. The first year of electronics at Douglas County High School had gone well — genuine aptitude, and I was going to graduate in 1975 with two full years of electronics training behind me. The decision made itself: electronics as a career, either as a technician or an engineer. Whatever it required.

That decision, made by a seventeen-year-old boy, in the dark of a moonless night with a three-legged dog and a spiral notebook, on a ten-acre horse property on Wolfensberger Road, eventually led to more than thirty-five years as a very successful Electrical Engineer: NSA headquarters at Fort Meade, the Johns Hopkins Applied Physics Laboratory in Laurel, and many covert defense programs, while employed by Honeywell, and an ASIC design now running in more than five million deployed systems worldwide. Every one of those outcomes traces, in a direct and unbroken line, back to a circle of Gamble Oak in the early morning hours of July 26, 1974.

With everything resolved, I gathered my things and took one last look up.

The Milky Way had moved.

An hour and a half earlier, it had been directly overhead, running north to south. Now it had shifted dramatically to the west, hovering perhaps five degrees above the Rampart Range — the long line of mountains forming the western horizon in Douglas County. My first instinct was to marvel at how far across the sky it had traveled while I was sitting there. And then, in the space of a single breath, the realization arrived with the force of something that should have been obvious all along:

The Milky Way had not moved. I had. I was standing on a tiny planet hurtling through space at a speed beyond any meaningful comprehension, carrying me along with it the entire time I had been sitting in that circle of oak writing in the dark, without a single sensation of motion, without any awareness whatsoever of what was actually happening beneath my feet every moment of every day.

In the exact moment that landed — the full, staggering, humbling scale of it — God spoke:

"There ya go, lad."

A warm breeze crossed my face.

Four words, and a warm breeze. That is all He said. But every problem I had carried with me down that hillside in those early morning hours — my broken heart, the world, my future, everything — was instantly, not gradually but instantly and completely, put into its proper proportion against the magnitude and glory of what God had just shown me. The Milky

Way above the Rampart Range. The planet spinning silently beneath my feet. The sheer, incomprehensible scale of creation, against which every problem I had arrived with was genuinely, objectively, cosmically small.

My life was never the same again.

Later that morning, when I woke up, the notebook came out again. I rewrote everything I had written in the dark — legibly this time, in the light of day, in readable sentences — and then read it all back to myself. The effect of seeing the full arc of that night laid out in readable form, from the love I had lost to the Milky Way, from the career decision to the warm breeze, is something I find difficult to fully describe, even now.

My mother remarked on the change later that same day. She looked at me with the calm certainty she brought to most things and said: “I don’t know what happened to you last night, but when I went to bed, you were a seventeen-year-old boy. Now you have the maturity and wisdom of a thirty-four-year-old man.”

She was right. She usually was.

Chapter 5

Gabriel

A few weeks after the night under the Gamble Oak — sometime in August of 1974, still that same extraordinary summer — my best friend, Ted Nelson, and I had been up all night at Daniels Park.

Daniels Park sits roughly halfway between Denver and Castle Rock, on a ridge above the Plum Creek Valley. It is one of those places in Colorado where the landscape does something to you regardless of the hour, but especially at sunrise, when the sun comes up behind you from the east and the Rampart Range stands in full relief to the west — hues of blue, green and red - definitely one of my favorite places on earth. We had been up the entire night, talking and watching the sky the way young men do when they are young enough to stay up all night without it costing them anything. By the time the eastern horizon began to lighten, I was standing at the edge of the ridge, facing west, watching the mountains emerge from the dark as the light built behind me.

The sun crept over the horizon. My long shadow stretched out before me, pointing west down the slope toward the Plum Creek Valley below. Everything was quiet in the way early morning is quiet before the world decides to begin — gathered, still, holding its breath.

Then I heard something.

Or almost heard something — which is the more precise description. It was like the sound of large wings landing, nearly inaudible, arriving immediately to my left. The kind of sound you almost convince yourself you imagined. But I did not imagine it.

And then an awareness arrived.

That word is chosen carefully, because awareness is exactly what it was. Not a visual event. Not something that could be pointed to or photographed or measured. A sudden and total awareness of presence — the way you know, in a quiet room, that someone has come in behind you before they speak or move. Except that what I was sensing was not merely a person. Not by any definition I had previously held for that word. Whatever was there existed in a category I had no name for.

There was no shadow. The sun was at my back, low on the eastern horizon. My own shadow ran out before me to the west, long and precise in the early light. To my left, where this presence stood, there was no shadow at all. Whatever was there existed in some relationship to light and to form that lay entirely outside the natural rules I had spent my life inside of.

Immense. The sense of scale was overwhelming. Twenty feet tall at minimum, by any approximation that could be made while keeping my gaze forward. Not frightening — this is important. Not threatening or dark. The quality of the presence was not threatening in any way. What it produced was awe in its oldest and most literal sense — the kind that makes you very still and very quiet and very certain that what is happening is real, and that the appropriate response is reverence rather than fear.

I did not turn to look. I stood still, facing the mountains, and I spoke to whatever was standing beside me.

“I don’t know who you are,” I said quietly, “or why you’re here... but thank you, very much, for your presence. I appreciate it very much!”

There was no verbal response. The presence simply was — vast and still and warm, the way a great fire is warm from across a room — and then, in time, it was gone. Not dramatically. Just gone, the way a fire goes when it has finished.

I stood there for a while afterward, looking at the mountains and the valley and the long shadow running west from my feet, holding the experience the way you hold something you know is important but do not yet have a container for.

The name came later, assembled from everything that followed over the course of a lifetime. From a message delivered in April of 2007 that pointed directly back to that morning on the ridge. From the full shape of a life in which this particular Archangel has appeared at least twice, separated by more than thirty years — once at the very beginning of my adult spiritual life, and once at the formal moment of my restoration.

Gabriel does not speak to me directly, as far as I know. He arrives. He is felt. He communicates through presence, through light, through other people, through the nearly inaudible sound of large wings on a Colorado morning. He is God's appointed messenger for the most significant formal communications in my life. And he was there at the very beginning of it — on that ridge above the Plum Creek Valley, at sunrise, casting no shadow, wordless and immense and warm, standing beside a seventeen-year-old boy who had no name for him but thanked him anyway.

Looking back across more than fifty years, that response — the gratitude offered to a presence I could not identify, for a visit whose purpose I did not yet understand — may have been exactly the right one.

Chapter 6

An Old Friend I Hadn't Seen in a While

Fifteen years passed between the night under the Gamble Oak and the morning in a chapel that I'm about to convey to you. Fifteen years of building a career, making choices, living the life that the decision made at seventeen had set in motion.

The engineering path was working exactly as planned. By the summer of 1988, I was thirty-one years old, living in the mountains west of Denver in a community called Hilldale Pines, in a house I had built on 1.6 acres in November of 1982. The career was taking off. The finances were in order. And a realization arrived that had been quietly building for some time: it was time to make good on the promise I had made to God at seventeen. If I was going to raise the best human beings I could, I needed to find a wife and start the family I had committed to building.

I will say this plainly, and without extended complaint: I was impatient, and I chose the wrong woman. Not the one God would have selected for me. I make no elaborate argument about this and assign no blame. God's plan is God's plan, and I was a willing participant in every choice I made. But the years that followed were years of genuine difficulty, and they are the subject of a later chapter. For now: I was engaged in the spring of 1989, and I brought the woman I planned to marry to Colorado Springs to meet my parents for the first time.

We attended Mass at the Catholic Chapel on the Air Force Academy campus — not the iconic chapel the campus is best known for, but a significantly more modest building. Still, there is something that accumulates in certain buildings over years of sincere petition. That chapel had it. You could feel it when you walked in.

I entered the pew where my parents were waiting, knelt to pray, and bowed my head. When I finished, I began to lift my head slowly — the way you do after genuine prayer, when you are not quite ready to be fully back in the world yet — my gaze moving first to the bottom of the crucifix above the altar, then upward along it, to the face of Christ. That is precisely when Jesus initiated a conversation with me.

"Where've you been?", Jesus asked, directly and conversationally — the way an old friend asks when he has not seen you in a while and he has genuinely noticed your absence. Not from a formal distance. Not in the liturgical register of a church service, with its appropriate reverence. He spoke the way someone speaks when they are glad to see you and are not going to pretend otherwise.

I answered without thinking, the way you answer someone you have already agreed to skip the formalities with.

"I know, I know," I said. "It's been a while since I've been in church—"

"No, no, no," Jesus said. "You're good. Just keep doing what you've been doing."

And then the Holy Spirit joined us.

What happened next lasted forty-five minutes. Weeping and laughing simultaneously — not from distress, not from confusion, but from the sheer, overwhelming presence of joy and love and peace in excess of what a human body can contain quietly. The Holy Spirit does not arrive in words. The Holy Spirit arrives as pure, undeniable presence — love and peace at a magnitude that simply cannot be held in silence. It comes out of you, whether you intend it to or not. Tears and laughter at the same time, which is bewildering to observe from the outside and is, from the inside, one of the most profoundly beautiful and disorienting experiences available to a human being.

Forty-five minutes of this. In front of my parents. In front of my fiancée. In front of dozens of people in the nearby pews who had arrived at the Air Force Academy chapel for Sunday Mass and were now watching a man weep and laugh for the better part of an hour, with no apparent explanation.

The specific content of what Jesus and I discussed that morning has faded the way the details of a long, warm reunion sometimes fade, leaving the quality of the encounter rather than a precise transcript. What has never faded, not for a single day in the thirty-seven years since, is how the exchange felt. The warmth of being completely known by someone. The ease of a relationship that requires no explanation because the history is already there and neither party has any doubt about the other.

"Where've you been?" Not an accusation. A question between friends. Already answered: "You're good. Just keep doing what you've been doing."

The word that most accurately describes what that morning established is one that surprises people in this context. The word is friendly. The relationship between Jesus and me, confirmed in that Catholic chapel on the Air Force Academy campus in Colorado Springs, is friendly. He spoke the way a close friend speaks — without formality, without distance, with complete familiarity, with genuine pleasure in the reunion. I understand that word will seem inadequate to some readers, and perhaps even irreverent to others. It is the accurate word, and there is no better one.

Chapter 7

The Years of Testing

My oldest son Adam was born on July 15, 1991. His two brothers followed in the years after. Three sons. The promise made to God on the night of July 26, 1974 had been answered, and I was determined — with everything I had — to honor my end of it.

What I had not fully accounted for was this: when you publicly declare your intention to raise God-centered children in a world that has a dedicated adversary who understands precisely what is at stake in the constant battle for the human soul, you, unfortunately, but definitively, draw attention to yourself. Specific, intentional, targeted, and Dark attention. I believe that is exactly what happened to my family beginning in the winter of 1992, when Adam was six months old.

From the time Adam was six months old until he was fourteen, my three sons and I were under what I can only describe as constant demonic assault. I use that language carefully, specifically, and without apology because it is the most accurate description. From the winter of 1992 forward, I was subjected to nearly constant physical, emotional, and psychological abuse, the source of which could only be described as demonic. The years that followed tested my faith, my finances, my legal standing, and my sanity — not because my faith broke, but because the system I turned to for justice proved itself to have no interest in providing it to any man in my position.

The Violence Against Women Act of 1989 is, in my direct lived experience, one of the most unconstitutional pieces of legislation in American history. Under its provisions, any accusation by any woman against any man required no evidence. The man was simply presumed to be guilty, from the outset. There was no longer the Constitutionally "guaranteed" rights of the Presumption of Innocence or Due Process and, due to the deliberate wording of the legislation itself, the courts gave the accused no realistic path to vindication. False accusations carried no legal consequence for the accuser. None whatsoever. The full weight of that system came down on me through the District Attorney's office, through the Douglas County Department of Health and Human Services, through agencies that insisted at every step that their every action was taken solely in the interest of my sons. The process drove me into bankruptcy as I attempted, in vain, to seek justice in a system that had structurally eliminated any mechanism for providing it to any man. Once bankrupt, every agency that had claimed to act on behalf of my sons disappeared without a word, without a follow-up, without so much as a phone call.

I have never forgotten that. It is foundational to my ongoing political activism on behalf of men's and fathers' rights, and I will continue to be an advocate on that front for as long as I have a voice. When people speak of "fatherless homes" in this country, they are very often describing, whether they know it or not, homes from which fathers were forcibly removed by exactly the mechanism I have just described. The father is not absent. He was expelled. That distinction is enormous. It is almost never made in public discourse. And the children who grow up in those homes, told in a hundred ways that their fathers chose to leave, deserve to have someone make that distinction clearly on their father's behalf.

In April of 1997, in the middle of all of it — the abuse, the legal persecution, the bankruptcy, the years of fighting a system that had decided in advance what the outcome would be - clearly one of the lowest and weakest times of my blessed life – I, regrettably, committed adultery.

I rationalized it to myself at the time as justified, even understandable, given everything I had endured. God was not impressed with my rationalization, at all. I knew that the moment I made the choice and then acted upon it.

The direct interaction I had experienced with God and the Holy Trinity since the afternoon on those stairs when I was ten years old — the conversations, the encounters, the clear and ongoing dialogue with the divine that had been the most precious constant of my entire life, the thing above all other things that defined who I was and how I moved through the world — stopped. Not gradually. Not partially. Stopped, completely.

God's love remained. I was still aware of it. But the direct presence, the clear dialogue, the immediate sense of communion with the Holy Trinity that I had lived inside since childhood — that was gone. The channel was closed. The frequency went silent. Where there had been a conversation, there was now only quiet. Deafening, palpable quiet.

God did not abandon me. He withdrew. Those are fundamentally different things, and the distinction matters. Abandonment leaves nothing — no awareness, no sense of presence, no sense of love. Withdrawal leaves the awareness of love and the absence of voice. In some ways, that is more instructive than abandonment, because it makes unmistakably clear exactly what has been lost and precisely why. There was no ambiguity about what had happened or what had caused it. A vow had been broken. God held me to it with the most precise instrument He had: He withdrew the one thing in my life I valued above all others. The accounting was exact. The justice was flawless. I had nothing to argue against it, because personal accountability had been the operating system of my relationship with God since I was twelve years old, and what it was now doing was simply operating. With perfect precision.

I had three sons I loved with everything in me, a career I had rebuilt piece by piece, and a silence where the voice of God had always been. I lived in that silence and I waited — without knowing how long the wait would be, without any indication of when or whether it would end.

Chapter 8

Forgiven

My first marriage officially ended in 2005. In late 2006, still carrying the hope of building the God-centered family I had promised to raise, I joined eHarmony. Within a few weeks, a woman reached out to me with an opening line that stopped me entirely: "Jesus told me to love you", she said.

I was flattered and deeply skeptical in equal measure — which is, I think, the appropriate response to that particular claim from a person you have just met. A person with a serious and long-standing relationship with God develops, over time, a finely calibrated ability to distinguish genuine divine encounter from wishful thinking, sincere self-deception, or something more deliberately manipulative. Her claim warranted serious consideration. It did not warrant immediate acceptance. So I kept my eyes and my discernment open as we began spending time together, paying close attention to what she knew and how she knew it.

After a while, I came to believe she was telling the truth. She described specific things about me — about my history with God, about the precise nature of what my relationship with the Holy Trinity had been, and about what had happened to it in April of 1997 — things that only God and I knew. Not things that could have been arrived at through research, or inference, or careful listening. She was operating as a channel for something real, whether she fully understood that role or not. Jesus had apparently made His intentions clear to her, and she had responded by reaching out to me on eHarmony. Stranger things have happened. In my experience, stranger things happen routinely.

In April of 2007, during a quiet evening at her house, she looked up with a mildly surprised expression — the expression of someone who has just noticed something unexpected — and said: "Oh — Gabriel is here and wanted to know if you had any questions for him."

As I was collecting my thoughts about what one might reasonably ask an Archangel, she spoke again.

"Gabriel has something to say to you. He wanted you to know that, in spite of God removing the path from you, you stayed on the path — and we noticed. We are very pleased with you. Your sins are forgiven."

Shortly after that, the direct relationship and dialogue with God and the Holy Trinity resumed. Right where it had left off in April of 1997 — the channel opened again, with the particular quality of a connection restored after a long separation, familiar and warm and immediately recognizable. Everything I had lived without was suddenly present again. The conversation that had defined my life for more than thirty years before April of 1997 simply, miraculously, continued.

And then I did the mathematics.

April of 1997 to April of 2007: exactly ten years. Gabriel's message of forgiveness had not arrived eleven months late or three months early. It had arrived on the precise ten-year anniversary of my transgression, to the month. The same Archangel who had stood beside me at Daniels Park at sunrise in August of 1974 — the immense, shadowless presence I had thanked without knowing his name — had been sent back to deliver the message of forgiveness on the exact day God had determined the accounting was complete.

Personal accountability. Two words. A vow violated in April of 1997. The consequence carried with absolute precision through ten years of silence. Forgiveness delivered through an Archangel on the precise anniversary of the transgression. This is God operating with the exactitude of a mathematician and the mercy of a father, simultaneously, in the life of one man who broke a promise and waited and was forgiven. Those two qualities — exactitude and mercy — are not in tension with each other. They are the same thing, expressed together, and I have never understood that more completely than I did in April of 2007.

It was in those same days that I came to understand something else. The immense presence felt standing beside me at Daniels Park at sunrise in August of 1974 — the being I had thanked without knowing his name, the one who cast no shadow and stood at least twenty feet tall in my awareness — had also been Gabriel. The same Archangel had been present at the very beginning of my adult spiritual life, in the summer of the year the promise was made. And he had returned at the formal moment of my restoration, ten years to the month after my failure. God assigns His messengers with intention and keeps meticulous track of where they have been and what they have been asked to do.

Years later, I remarried. During a heated argument in that marriage — the kind of argument that sometimes cracks things open and lets the truth out ahead of schedule — my wife said: "If God hadn't told me to marry you, I never would have!"

I asked what she meant by that. She described a specific morning, sometime after we had started dating. I had gotten out of bed and gone into the kitchen. Suddenly, without warning, the entire kitchen filled with an incredibly bright light. Not a natural light, not the light of the morning sun coming through the windows. Something else entirely. In her mind, the name Gabriel consumed all other thought. She experienced it as overwhelming, as unmistakable, and she took it as a sign that God wanted her to marry me. And so she did. She had never told me about this before that moment in the argument. It came out the way certain things come out during arguments — like something that had been waiting for a sufficient crack in the conversation to escape through.

Gabriel again. Filling a kitchen with light on an ordinary Colorado morning, confirming a woman in a decision about a man God apparently still had plans for. The same Archangel. The same signature — overwhelming presence, experienced not in words but in light and in the immediate certainty of what that light means. Present at the beginning, present at the restoration, and present again quietly in a kitchen on a morning I was not even aware of, at the time.

He is faithful, this messenger. I am grateful for every appearance he has made in my life, including — perhaps especially — the ones I did not know about until years after they happened.

Chapter 9

The Language of Numbers

I was born on June 9th, 1957 — the ninth day of the sixth month, the third son of my father. The numbers were present at the beginning, signed into the date of my arrival before I had any awareness of them or any reason to look for them.

Throughout my adult life — for as long as I can remember and when I am consciously listening to God, not driven by my own thoughts, weakness and rationalizations — I have noticed something. When I am moving in the right direction. When God is confirming a path, compelling me toward something, or affirming that I am exactly where I am supposed to be, doing precisely what He has planned for me, a noticeable pattern has emerged. In those moments, when I happen to glance at a clock, check a temperature gauge, look at a cell phone battery percentage, catch a receipt total, or notice a license plate — the numbers I see, whether read as presented or reduced by addition to a single digit, consistently resolve to values divisible by 3, 6, or 9. The number 9 carries the most significant weight.

I do not arrange my day around the clock. I do not go looking for these alignments or engineer them. I live my life and notice what the numbers say when I happen to look. The pattern has held across decades, across thousands of individual observations, across the full range of contexts and circumstances that a life presents. I am an electrical engineer. I think in systems. I look for signal in noise, and I have learned across a long career to distinguish a genuine pattern from coincidence, wishful thinking, or confirmation bias. I know what each of those looks like. This is a genuine pattern.

God speaks to me in the language of a man whose mind naturally operates in systems, precision, and measurable signal. He speaks to an engineer in the language an engineer will notice and recognize. That is not a small thing. It is a very specific, very personal form of attention — the kind that tells you the One communicating has studied who you are and is choosing accordingly.

Nikola Tesla was perhaps the greatest electrical engineer who ever lived. That is not a casual claim. The alternating current that powers your home, the electromagnetic principles underlying wireless transmission, the polyphase motor, the Tesla coil, the foundations of the electrical infrastructure of the modern world — all of it traces back, in some fundamental way, to Tesla's mind. He was a man of extraordinary perceptual sensitivity and almost superhuman intellectual precision, capable of designing complete three-dimensional mechanical systems in his mind before building them, and building them exactly as he had imagined.

He was also, throughout his life, consumed by the numbers 3, 6, and 9 in a way his contemporaries found entirely baffling and could not explain.

He walked around a block three times before entering a building. He stayed only in hotel rooms whose numbers were divisible by three. He used exactly eighteen napkins at every meal — eighteen, which reduces digitally to nine. He is widely reported to have washed his hands a compulsive number of times throughout the day, always in groups of three. He structured significant portions of his daily life around these three numbers with what looked to outside observers like obsessive-compulsive behavior, but was, I believe, something considerably more precise than that. Tesla was not a man given to irrational behavior. He was one of the most rational minds in the history of engineering. What he was doing, I think, was following a pattern he had detected in the structure of reality itself — a pattern he could feel with the intuition of a genius even when he could not yet fully explain it through mathematics or physics.

He once said: "If you only knew the magnificence of the 3, 6 and 9, then you would have a key to the universe."

He was not being poetic. He was being precise. He was pointing at something he believed was real and fundamental, and inviting anyone with sufficient perception to look.

Modern mathematics offers a partial explanation through what is called digital root theory. In the base-ten number system, if you take the doubling sequence — 1, 2, 4, 8, 16, 32, 64, 128 — and reduce each number to its digital root by summing its digits until you arrive at a single digit, you get an endlessly repeating cycle: 1, 2, 4, 8, 7, 5, 1, 2, 4, 8, 7, 5. Six numbers, rotating forever without variation. What you notice immediately is what is absent: 3, 6, and 9 never appear anywhere in that cycle. They exist entirely outside of it. They form their own closed, self-referential system — a signal running alongside the primary mathematical structure of the base-ten world without ever intersecting it. Multiples of 9 always reduce back to 9: 18 reduces to 9, 27 reduces to 9, 36 reduces to 9, and so on without exception. Multiples of 3 and 6 always reduce to 3, 6, or 9 and cycle among themselves. Mathematically, they are a separate family entirely. A pattern within the pattern. A closed loop running on a frequency different from everything else in the system.

Tesla saw this and spent his life trying to understand what it meant through physics and engineering. He could feel its importance the way a great engineer feels when a system is behaving in a way that indicates something fundamental has not yet been understood. He could not always articulate the full theory. But he was completely certain of the phenomenon, and he followed it faithfully across an entire lifetime.

Here is what I make of the convergence between Tesla's observations and my own.

Tesla was a man of extraordinary perceptual gifts who arrived at 3, 6, and 9 through mathematical observation and engineering intuition — through the language of numbers and physics. I am an electrical engineer who arrived at the same three numbers through direct divine communication, observed and calibrated over decades of attentive living. Two instruments. Two entirely different approaches. The same signal.

I am not claiming Tesla had a relationship with God equivalent to mine, or that he understood the pattern in the same way I understand it. Tesla was not a conventionally religious man. What he was is a man who believed the universe operated according to mathematical principles most people could not yet perceive, and who followed what he could detect with the discipline and precision of a great engineer. He saw something real. He said so plainly. And the three numbers he kept arriving at are the same three numbers God has used to speak confirmation and direction into my daily life for six decades, signed into my birth date before I knew to look for them.

That convergence is worth sitting with carefully. I have sat with it for years. I do not have a complete explanation for it, and I will not manufacture one. What I have is the observation itself: the greatest electrical engineer who ever lived spent his life fixated on 3, 6, and 9 and said they were a key to the universe. I have been receiving those same numbers as the language of divine communication, and synchronization, for my entire adult life.

Two instruments, pointed at the same thing, from entirely different directions.

For the reader who finds direct divine encounter too large a step to take all at once — here is a bridge. You know Tesla. You know what he was capable of, and you know he was serious when he pointed at something and said it mattered. He pointed at 3, 6, and 9. I have spent fifty-eight years receiving those same numbers as the language of a God who knows I am an engineer and communicates accordingly.

God speaks in whatever language will reach you. For Tesla, it was mathematics. For a man trained in electrical engineering who was also visited by an Archangel at sunrise and made promises to God under a sky full of stars in the Colorado dark — it is both at once, and has been for as long as I can remember.

Chapter 10

Adam

A request, before this chapter begins: sit with it.

Not because it is difficult to read — though it may be. But because what happened in the years surrounding my son Adam's passing contains the most important thing I know about God, about the nature of faith under the most extreme conditions a human life can present, and about what it means to be held, across more than four decades, to a promise and a caveat made under a Colorado sky at seventeen years old.

Adam was my oldest son. He was born on July 15, 1991. From the day he arrived, I loved him with everything I had — with the specific, weighted love that a father reserves for his firstborn, the one who makes him a father for the first time, the one who changes everything simply by arriving. He was the first answer to the promise made to God on that early morning in July of 1974. The first of the children asked for and committed to raising well. He grew into an extraordinary young man, brilliant, mature, and gifted beyond his years. His two younger brothers, Austin, and Andrew (Drew), and I were, and are, deeply proud of him, in all the ways that actually matter.

On February 18, 2018, Adam passed from this world in a car accident. He was twenty-six years old.

When I received the news, I fell to my knees.

And what came out of me — immediately, involuntarily, without any conscious intention or forethought whatsoever — was this:

"Of course it was Adam."

I had no idea what those words meant when I said them. None. They arrived ahead of understanding, the way certain things do in the most extreme moments of a life — a truth the conscious mind has not yet assembled, spoken before it can be reasoned through or examined. I heard myself say them and could not have told you, in that moment, what they meant or where they came from.

For more than five years after Adam passed, I could not look at a photograph of my son. That is not a figure of speech. It is not a poetic way of describing grief. It is a precise statement of fact. A man who had spoken with Jesus. Who had been moved by the Holy Spirit until he wept and laughed for forty-five minutes in a Catholic chapel. Who had lived in ongoing, intimate awareness of God's presence for more than fifty years. That man could not look at a picture of his son who had left this world. Not from anger at God — there was no anger at God. Not from a failure of faith. The loss was simply too great. Adam's face, in a photograph, was more than I could carry.

I loved God. I trusted God. I simply could not look at any pictures of Adam.

More than five years after Adam passed, God reminded me of something.

In that early morning in July of 1974. In the circle of Gamble Oak on Wolfensberger Road. The spiral notebook on my lap, full of everything I had emptied out of my mind. The promise made — and specifically, precisely, the caveat I had attached to it before God and no one else:

“God, please never take any of my children from me, because I don’t think I could deal with losing a child.”

I had meant every word of it. Sitting under those stars at seventeen, I had believed it completely and without reservation. I had told God the one thing I was not strong enough to survive.

And He showed me I was wrong.

In the moment that reminder arrived, the words spoken while falling to my knees on February 18, 2018 finally opened into meaning. Of course it was Adam. Of course it was the firstborn, the oldest, the one carried with the particular weight of love that a father carries his first child. Of course it was the one whose loss I had specifically, explicitly, and with complete sincerity told God I could not survive.

Not random. Not arbitrary. Not punishment for anything I had done or failed to do. The precise and faithful fulfillment of a covenant made on a Colorado hillside in 1974, witnessed and held in memory by the God who had been listening to every word of it that night. Adam was not taken as punishment. His passing was permitted to demonstrate — with the completeness and the finality that only the most devastating possible proof can provide — that there is nothing, no loss, no grief, no devastation anywhere in the range of human experience, that cannot be survived through God's love. The very thing I had declared unsurvivable was the thing God used to show me, beyond any conceivable doubt, that it could be survived. That with Him, anything can be survived.

The evidence was right in front of me. More than five years of waking up every morning under the full, undiminished weight of Adam's absence — and still standing. Still praying. Still here. Not without pain — the pain is real, and it is permanent, and it will always be mine, and ours. But the pain and the faith coexisted, as they are capable of doing when faith is genuine and God is faithful. I was surviving the unsurvivable, through exactly the means God had always offered: His love, His presence, and His faithfulness to a covenant that neither of us had forgotten, even across forty-four years.

When that understanding arrived, I was able, for the first time since February 18, 2018, to look at a photograph of my first-born son.

God had also shown me his beautiful and divine Grace years earlier when, just before I went out to give

Adam's eulogy at his memorial service, God spoke to me. In essence, what He said was this: I gave you that wonderful son for twenty-six years. Now go out there and eulogize him.

So I did. I walked to that podium and I said what needed to be said, in front of everyone who had loved Adam, and I honored his life in a way I hope was worthy of him. I could not have done it without those words in the moments before I walked out. What God gave me in those seconds was everything I needed to stand upright in the hardest moment of my life and do the thing that was required of me.

I am grateful for that beyond what I can adequately express.

Here is what I need to say to you, from the deepest and most costly place available to me:

Do not put caveats around your profession of faith, ever.

I mean that exactly, practically, and from direct personal experience. When you make a promise to God, make it clean. Do not attach conditions to it. Do not name the thing you cannot bear. Do not tell God what you are not strong enough to survive, because whatever you declare unsurvivable may be precisely what He uses to demonstrate the full and sufficient depth of His love. Not as punishment. Not as cruelty. As the most complete and unmistakable possible proof that His love reaches exactly as far as you feared it might not.

I know this because I lived it. I survived the thing I told God I could not survive. And I did not survive it alone — I was carried through it, accompanied in it, held in it, by the God who had been listening on the night I made the promise, and on the night I added the caveat, and on every night between that night and the February morning when Adam left. Not spared the grief. Not rescued from the pain. Carried through both. That is the promise He makes and that He keeps: not that He will prevent the loss, but that He will be present in it.

He was present with me. He is present now. He will be present with you, too, in whatever you are carrying. I am as certain of that as I am of anything I have set down in this book.

Epilogue

God Speaks to You, Too

Everything in this book happened.

A ten-year-old stopped on a staircase by the Holy Spirit and commanded to make a gun safe before re-entering a room. A twelve-year-old designing a comparative religious studies curriculum and arriving, with a room full of seventh and eighth graders, at the two words that define man's relationship with God. A seventeen-year-old emptying his mind onto paper under a Colorado sky and hearing God say, "There ya go, lad," as a warm breeze crossed his face. An Archangel at sunrise on a ridge above the Plum Creek Valley, casting no shadow. Jesus in a Catholic chapel on the Air Force Academy campus asking, "Where've you been?" with the ease of an old friend who is glad to see you. The Holy Spirit making it impossible to sit quietly in a pew for forty-five minutes. A vow broken, a ten-year silence, forgiveness delivered through an Archangel on the precise anniversary of the transgression. A promise made at seventeen, fulfilled in the most devastating and the most transformative way imaginable, pointing to the only truth that made complete sense of any of it: that nothing — not even the thing declared unsurvivable — falls outside the reach of God's love.

None of this happened to an extraordinary person. It happened to an engineer from Denver who grew up in an Irish-Catholic household on South Xavier Street, made serious mistakes, worked hard, deeply loved his sons, and paid attention. The paying attention is the part that matters most. God has been speaking for the entirety of my life. The encounters in this book were not rare exceptions granted to a uniquely favored individual. They were what happens when you are genuinely present in your own life and willing to say plainly what you experience, without softening it into metaphor or qualifying it into meaninglessness.

Our culture has trained us to do exactly that — to soften and qualify. To say "I had a strange feeling" rather than "God was present." To frame encounters in the passive, deniable language of coincidence rather than the direct language of relationship. To keep the most significant experiences of our lives in a private compartment where they cannot be examined, questioned, or shared — because we are not sure we would be believed, or because the institutions that were supposed to provide a framework for these experiences positioned themselves as required intermediaries instead. That silence has cost us something real, individually and collectively, and it has left a great many people alone with experiences that are genuine, significant, and completely without community.

This book is permission to stop being silent about what you know is true. God speaks to me. He speaks to you, too. You are not alone in what you have experienced. You are not deluded or guilty of wishful thinking. You have been met, and the encounter was real, and you are allowed to say so.

If you have walked away from organized religion but have not walked away from God — you are making a distinction that is entirely correct. God exists completely outside every institution ever built in His name. He was here before all of them. Direct access to Him requires no intermediary, no membership, no doctrinal subscription, and no building. It requires honesty, personal accountability, and a genuine willingness to be present in your own life with enough attention to notice when He is speaking.

If you are sitting in grief right now, in the particular darkness that follows losing someone you loved beyond what you thought you could bear — hear this as directly as I know how to say it: He is with you in it. Not observing from a safe distance. Not managing your situation from elsewhere. In it, with you, right now. He carried me through losing my first born son. I told you that story so you would know that the carrying is real, and available, and not contingent on your having earned it.

If you have had a direct encounter — heard something, felt something, been stopped in your tracks by something that had no natural explanation — and you have never told another person because you were not sure it was real, or because you were not sure you would be believed: it was real. Say so. The saying of it is part of the faithfulness.

Two words. Personal accountability. There is a God, and every one of us is personally accountable to Him for what we do with the life He gave us. That is the whole of it. That has always been the whole of it, across every century and every culture in which human beings have tried to understand their relationship with the divine.

God speaks to me.

He speaks to you, too.

He always has.

Thank You, God.

About the Author

Patrick J. Delohery is a retired electrical engineer and entrepreneur living in Colorado Springs, Colorado. Over a thirty-five-year career in defense, intelligence, and commercial engineering, he worked at NSA Headquarters at Fort Meade, Maryland and the Johns Hopkins Applied Physics Laboratory in Laurel, Maryland, both while on assignment through Honeywell, as well as at the National Anti-Submarine Warfare Fleet Headquarters. His first ASIC design runs in more than five million deployed systems worldwide. He is a named inventor on multiple U.S. and foreign patents.

He is the founder of EPIC AI Business Solutions, LLC, and the author of Three Very Short Stories: God, Guns and Grace. Growing Up In America. Book 1, available on Amazon.

He is the father of three sons. He dedicates this book to the oldest, Adam.

Acknowledgments

This book was organized and shaped with the assistance of Ben, an AI writing collaborator I built and trained — customized specifically for this project on Claude, by Anthropic. The accounts, the theology, and every word that matters are mine. Ben helped with the architecture, writing the connective tissue, and maintaining the structure — freeing me to focus on the memoir itself.

Cover photograph by Evgenit, Pixabay License. Free for commercial use; no attribution required. Pixabay.com.

www.ingramcontent.com/pod-product-compliance
Lightning Source LLC
LaVergne TN
LVHW090535110826
845146LV00003B/1112